W9-CHK-779

# I Can Show Respect

## Doing the Right Thing

Written by Jenette Donovan Guntly
Illustrated by Kathi Ember

GARETH STEVENS
GS
PUBLISHING
A World Almanac Education Group Company

Please visit our web site at: www.garethstevens.com
For a free color catalog describing Gareth Stevens Publishing's list of high-quality books
and multimedia programs, call 1-800-542-2595 (USA) or 1-800-387-3178 (Canada).
Gareth Stevens Publishing's fax: (414) 332-3567.

Library of Congress Cataloging-in-Publication Data

Guntly, Jenette Donovan.
    (Following the rules)
    I can show respect / written by Jenette Donovan Guntly; illustrated by Kathi Ember.
       p. cm. — (Doing the right thing)
    ISBN 0-8368-4248-0 (lib. bdg.)
    1. Respect—Juvenile literature.  I. Ember, Kathi.  II. Title.
  BJ1533.R4G86   2004
  179′.9—dc22                                      2004045296

This North American edition first published in 2005 by
**Gareth Stevens Publishing**
A World Almanac Education Group Company
330 West Olive Street, Suite 100
Milwaukee, WI  53212  USA

This edition copyright © 2005 by Gareth Stevens, Inc.  Original edition copyright © 2002 by Creative Teaching Press, Inc.,
P.O. Box 2723, Huntington Beach, CA  92647-0723.  First published in the United States in 2002 as *Following the Rules:
Learning about Respect* by Creative Teaching Press, Inc.  Original text copyright © 2002 by Regina G. Burch.

Illustrator: Kathi Ember
Gareth Stevens designer: Kami M. Koenig

All rights to this edition reserved to Gareth Stevens, Inc.  No part of this book may be reproduced, stored in a retrieval system,
or transmitted in any form or by any means, electronic, mechanical, photocopying, recording, or otherwise, without the prior
written permission of the publisher, except for the inclusion of brief quotations in an acknowledged review.

Printed in the United States of America

1 2 3 4 5 6 7 8 9 08 07 06 05 04

I can show respect!

I say please and thank you.

As I leave, I say goodbye.

When I'm talking to my friends,

I look them in the eye.

I follow the directions.

I obey the signs.

I use my indoor voice at school

and wait my turn in lines.

I listen to my teacher.

I'm fair when I play games.

I think before I speak and act.

I don't call people names.

If I treat others courteously,
then they will show respect for me.